LOSING KATY

LOSING KATY

A Memoir of Love, Loss, and Living Grief

Jackie L. Disch

BOOKLOGIX
Alpharetta, GA

The author has recounted events, locations, and conversations to the best of her ability. The author has made every effort to give credit to the source of any images, quotes, or other material contained within and obtain permissions when feasible.

No generative AI was used in the conceptualization, planning, drafting, or creative writing of this work. No permission is given for the use of this material for AI training purposes.

Human Authored™, Reg #: 7873765, https://authorsguild.org/human

Copyright © 2025 by Jackie L. Disch

All rights reserved. No part of this book may be reproduced or transmitted in any form or by any means, electronic or mechanical, including photocopying, recording, or any information storage and retrieval system, without permission in writing from the author.

ISBN: 978-1-6653-1048-2 - Paperback
eISBN: 978-1-6653-1049-9 - eBook

These ISBNs are the property of BookLogix for the express purpose of sales and distribution of this title. The content of this book is the property of the copyright holder only. BookLogix does not hold any ownership of the content of this book and is not liable in any way for the materials contained within. The views and opinions expressed in this book are the property of the Author/Copyright holder, and do not necessarily reflect those of BookLogix.

Library of Congress Control Number: 2025912562

∞This paper meets the requirements of ANSI/NISO Z39.48-1992 (Permanence of Paper)

Pema Chödrön quote used with permission of SoundsTrue
Simon, Tami. "The Breath of Compassion: Pema Chödrön." Awaken, August 26, 2020.
https://awaken.com/2020/08/the-breath-of-compassion-pema-chodron/.

Front cover photo of Katy at Lake Superior 2015 by Jackie L. Disch
Author photo by Scott Sater Photography

090225

In Honor of Katy (1950–2020)
who brought such love, laughter, and joy
into my life. You forever have my heart.

CONTENTS

Introduction — xi

June–December 2020

Dark Circles	3
No Longer Conscious	4
Writings to Katy	5
Rainstorms and Rainbows	6
The Great Barrier Grief	8
No One Allowed	9
Just Being Us	11
Trying to Make Sense	12
With Regard to the Needs of Others	13
Weighted Blanket	14
Three Months of Fridays	16
Standing on My Own	17
Surreal	18
Truth Is	19
I Hope You Know	20
Me without You	21

January–June 2021

A Few More Moments	25
The Memory of Our Time	26
I Would Have to Be	27
No Part of This Is Easy	28
The Transformative Work of Grief	29
She Holds Me Up	30
Magical Thinking	31
Over to You	32
Nonetheless	33
Moments	34
She Stays with Me	35

Tender Day	36
What I Don't Have	37
Barren Land	38
Lifeline	39

July–December 2021

Year One	43
Left Undone	44
Our Signal	45
Small Things	46
That In-between Place	47
Resting	48
Each Day	49
Witnessing Her Last Breath	50
Every Time	51
I Know How This Song Ends	52
Unmoored	53
Her Voice	54
Last and First	55
When You Were Real	56
Doing Things Alone	57
Loved	58
Even After	60

January–June 2022

A Found List Poem	63
Grief	64
Thanks for Asking	65
No Fair	66
Time Zones	67
How I Know	68
A Place to Land	69
Come Home	70
Surprise Passenger	71
Four Words	72

When Grief Induces Silence	73
The Failure of Language	74
Why I Stopped	75
Blazing Truth	76
Momentary Reprieve	77

July–December 2022

Everything's Changed	81
Lake Harriet	82
The Constant Questions	83
Since You've Gone	84
I Feel	85
The Comfort of You	86
Unwilling to Land	87
Grief Event	88
Living and Dying	89
Next Time	90
Empty Mess	91
Then, Now, Always	92
Living Grief	93
What If It Is	94
Sense and Senseless	95
Your Phone	96
All the Ways	97
What It Has Always Been	98
Grief Does Not Expire	99
She Said	100
Through the Fog	101

January–July 2023

Life	105
Because	106
Some Days	107
Negotiating New Spaces	109
No Other Word	110

Retreat	111
Only Me	112
Selfish Questions	114
Many More	115
The Projector of Grief	116
Gratitude	118
The Nature of Loss	119
Moving	120
Losing Katy	121
Notes and Acknowledgments	*125*

INTRODUCTION

Losing Katy: A Memoir of Love, Loss, and Living Grief is about my wife's death. It is a story that exemplifies our life together, the love we shared, and having to say goodbye.

The story is told through a collection of my writings from just before, during, and after Katy's death. It ends on the third-year anniversary. The writings are in chronological order, with dates included. I chose this layout to show how grief is not linear, how it can twist and turn when you least expect it.

There are recurring themes throughout the book; this is intentional only because it is the nature of grief. Feelings, thoughts, emotions, and experiences of all kinds show up at any time, repeatedly.

I have experienced many losses in my life—friends who died way too young, the deaths of my mother and father, and of Katy's parents—to name a few. I have been with people at the end of their lives. I have also studied death, dying, and end-of-life issues. But none of that prepared me for Katy's death.

Her death hit me on a level I did not realize existed. Because of that, I learned new things about grief. Mostly, I learned what it means to *live* grief, to be one with it. And I learned the ways that grief is an extension of our love for the one we lost. It walks with us, it ages with us "like a necessary guest you need to accommodate."

Losing Katy is an example of living grief. It shows the everyday experiences and nuances of grief. I invite you to walk with me through the pages of our story.

—Jackie

In the end, that's what we all need more than anything else: to be there for each other, in every kind of situation.
—*Pema Chödrön*

JUNE – DECEMBER

2020

DARK CIRCLES

The dark circles under my eyes
are not from lack of sleep—
sleeping is the "easier" part.

No, the dark circles under my eyes
are from grief—and deep,
unadulterated heartache.

June 12, 2020

NO LONGER CONSCIOUS

oh my god
how I miss you already

                                                                                     June 30, 2020

WRITINGS TO KATY

Katy, my sweetie—

I'm having separation anxiety. Much like you experience separating from your body during death, I feel a similar separation from out here. Your body has separated from me. It's causing me great anxiety.

What was I thinking letting you go without me?! There's nothing to keep me here. You were the best part of my life. You were the best part of me.

I can't even believe how much I miss you. I knew I would, but I entirely misjudged what it would feel like to have you gone. Then again, how would I know? No one like you has died before.

Today I did all the things we used to do. I got the house ready for the cleaner. I mowed the lawn. I picked up our usual Thursday evening dinner. And now I'm in bed. But you're not here. Well, you *are* here, but not physically, in the way I was used to, in the way you were for all those years.

How can you not be here?

July 18, 2020

RAINSTORMS AND RAINBOWS

I was sitting on the bed with Katy, listening to what would be her last few breaths, when suddenly I heard what sounded like hail pounding on the roof. It turned out to be big, plump raindrops.

I was excited because I knew how much Katy loved the sound of rain.

"Sweetie!" I exclaimed as I flung myself off the bed. "I think it's raining!"

I was so happy because I thought it would be peaceful for Katy to hear; that it would bring her joy and comfort.

It reminds me now of the first rainstorm I ever really listened to. It was a late afternoon summer storm. We climbed onto the bed to listen, as Katy told me how much she loved the sound and smell of rain, the rumble of thunder. I, on the other hand, was afraid of storms, especially high winds and lightning.

But that day, it was a gentle storm. As we lay listening to and experiencing the sounds, I felt a deep sense of safety, of belonging, and so very much love for the woman next to me.

It is one of my favorite first memories with her.

On the day Katy died, just as she took her last breath, a steady downpour came, along with some gentle thunder. No wind. No lightning.

The timing was impeccable.

In fact, no rain or storms were forecasted that day. It seemed to have come out of nowhere and lasted only a few minutes.

I believe it was Katy leaving.

The accompanying rainbow told me she was okay.

July 18, 2020

THE GREAT BARRIER GRIEF

It feels like there is
a barrier in my brain

It shelters me
from feeling the full
debilitating grief
I know is there

Allowing the precise
amount through
that I can tolerate

and still breathe.

August 9, 2020

NO ONE ALLOWED

"I'm not afraid of dying," Katy declared.

She was afraid of the ER, the hospital, the doctor—or anyone else—putting her there against her will.

She did not want to be left alone in one of those places, unable to communicate fully on her own. She was already trapped by her mind. She did not want to be trapped in a hospital or rehab or a nursing home, as well— away from me, away from our life together. She trusted me to be her voice.

COVID-19 policies dictated "No One Allowed."

Katy was not alone in her way of thinking. The COVID policies affected us all. Like everyone else, we had both heard on the news about people unable to be with their loved ones in a hospital or similar settings. As a result, people were dying alone— without family or friends or significant others by their sides.

Katy did not want to die alone.

Some solace was found in the overworked medical staff—on the front lines of this pandemic assault— who stood in for family, friends, loved ones— as witnesses when death came.

There were also many stories of people forgoing treatment so they could stay at home. Even if it meant hastening their death.

It takes courage to choose death graciously.

It takes courage to say NO when
those around you want you to stay.

Katy was exhausted. She was done.
She wanted peace. She wanted "out"
of the mind and body that now
held her captive.

That was the greatest gift we could
all give her—as painful as it was
to give.

August 15, 2020

JUST BEING US

Last night was the first time Katy appeared
in a dream since she died.

It had nothing to do with her death.
It was just Katy and me,
being us, together.

I woke up feeling happy. Then I realized
Katy was not next to me. Reality came
creeping back in.

But my heart remained happy, having
had the reminder of Katy and me
just being us, together—
both alive, both living.

It gave me hope that there is more than
just tears to be had.

I felt Katy in my heart.
I felt her with me again.

Just us, together.

August 22, 2020

TRYING TO MAKE SENSE

My mind is trying to make sense of it all.

Katy was here.
Now she is not.

For the first time in nearly a quarter century,
I am alone again.

But I am not the same.

Katy gave me a life like none I had ever expected.
We were at our best together.

I knew love with her.
And, with her, I knew how to love.
I knew happiness like no other; we shared that.

So many people have told me, since Katy's death,
how lucky we were to have found that kind of love;
not everyone does.

I realize we were fortunate.

But now, my mind is muddled,
like a child learning object permanence.

Here but not here.
Gone but not gone.

Can both be true?

Neither my mind nor my heart
is certain.

August 22, 2020

WITH REGARD TO THE NEEDS OF OTHERS

I cannot tend to you.

My own grief
takes up my nights
and days
and all space
in between
the cells of
my being.

My own grief
makes me selfish
in the eyes
of others—
and in my own
heart.

For that is what grief is:
all consuming
for the needs of Self.

Leaving no room
with regard to the needs of others.

September 3, 2020

WEIGHTED BLANKET

After an earlier night of terror dreams,
you asked for a weighted blanket. Actually,
you drew one as you tried to tell me
what you wanted.

In an effort to make me fully
understand, you gave me the name
of someone you said knew a lot about them.

By the end of the day, you had one.

I helped you cover yourself with the
blanket. It felt good, you said. It
helped you feel safe.

You stayed under its cover for a while.
Later, you moved it to the end of the bed.

That night, as we lay talking face
to face, in the best language you
had at the time—and through our
tears—you told me:

You wanted me to use the blanket
whenever I need to feel you close,
that it will protect and comfort me.

It was such a loving thing for you
to do. There you were, getting ready
to die, and you were looking for ways
to comfort me after you were gone.

It was an act of astounding love.

Thank you, Katy. Thank you for
giving me something of yourself
so concrete I can wrap myself
in it and know it is filled with
your love and comfort.

September 4, 2020

THREE MONTHS OF FRIDAYS

Three months of Fridays
have already passed

Leaving me
submerged in grief

Each day brings
a thousand little deaths

Sinking me
into widowhood.

September 26, 2020

STANDING ON MY OWN

I am like a toddler
the first time
they stand on their own.

The first time
of holding on to nothing,
no one holding on to them.

And that first moment
of realization comes—
filled with triumph, excitement,
pure joy at their accomplishment.

Standing on their own.

Then the next
realization hits—
filled with fear, uncertainty,
pure terror at what they just did.

And down they go.

Sometimes landing softly and laughing.
Sometimes landing hard and crying.

I am in the toddler
stage of grief—
but I cry when I realize
I am standing on my own.

September 28, 2020

SURREAL

That I make it through each day
without you by my side
That I take care of what needs
to be done
when I shouldn't be able to
move at all

is surreal

I don't know what keeps me standing
what keeps me going
without you

There is no reason

This life without you
is not real

It can't be.

November 16, 2020

TRUTH IS

You used to say you worried
about being older than me.
You were afraid you would
slow me down
or hold me back.

Truth is

You only ever filled me up.

November 21, 2020

I HOPE YOU KNOW

Do you know the happiness you brought me?
Do you know how you filled me up
and built me up and held me up
with your love and kindness,
your unwavering acceptance?
Your presence in my life gave me life.
I miss you every single day you are gone,
but I also hope you know
all the gifts you gave me.

December 24, 2020

ME WITHOUT YOU

It's Christmas Eve
and I'm waiting
for the tears to come.

I made it through
most of today
without them.

But the afternoon is fading
and my tears are waiting
as another evening
without you
descends.

It doesn't need to be a holiday
for me to miss you.
The tears, they come
whenever they wish.

I only want you here with me.

Because me without you
is just not right.

December 24, 2020

JANUARY – JUNE

2021

A FEW MORE MOMENTS

Katy was in bed with me last night.
I woke up to grab my water bottle
for a drink and thought, *Shhhhh—careful!
Don't wake Katy up!*
I truly felt she was behind me
on her side of the bed, sleeping on
her back, gently breathing.
I could physically feel her.
I was so happy! I thought, *What if she
really is there?* So, I snuck a look.
She wasn't there.
I turned back and took my drink
of water.
Then I knew she had left.
I couldn't sense her anymore.
But what a wonderful experience
it was—
to spend a few more moments
with my sweetie.

January 4, 2021

THE MEMORY OF OUR TIME

The time we got to
spend together
was the best part
of each day.

We lived for that time.
And that time
filled our lives.

What am I supposed to do
now that she is gone?

What does that leave me
to live for?

The memory of our time together
is not enough.

January 21, 2021

I WOULD HAVE TO BE

Katy kept asking
if I was going to be all right.
She worried about me,
worried for me.

I struggled to answer her.
I wanted to scream, "NO!"

But if now was the time
for her to go, then I would be okay.

I had to be. I did not want to be the one
keeping her here, making her stay for me,
without regard for her.

And I did not want to lie.

I wanted to give her
what she wanted/needed—
as no one else in her life
could, or would, or had before.

So, I said yes.
I would be all right.
For her—for us—I would have to be.

February 3, 2021

NO PART OF THIS IS EASY

No part of this is easy.

And if it looks
or seems easy
it is because of what
I have learned
from you, my love.

Being beside you
as you died taught me
how to have the strength
to do difficult things.

But let no one
mistake strength
for *ease*—
or ease
for *being okay*
with any part of this.

February 9, 2021

THE TRANSFORMATIVE WORK OF GRIEF

It is hard to change painful memories
into thankfulness for the time we had together.

It is hard to fill the void
and turn it into knowing she is always with me.

Yet that is the transformative
work of grief—

turning what was
into what still is.

February 28, 2021

SHE HOLDS ME UP

When Katy died,
my world exploded—
revealing the depth of our relationship
and the magnitude of my loss.

She was my protector,
my anchor, a piece of me.

She brought safety,
comfort, a peace of mind.

She knew
the deepest, most private places in me.

She brought out
the brightest, strongest light in me.

I am lost without her
yet she helps steer my way.

She holds me up
while grief consumes me.

March 6, 2021

MAGICAL THINKING

I think of the places
we used to live
and the places we went
to get away

And I think
> If I could just move back there
> or go visit that place
> I would find you
> alive and well

And we would be together again.

March 15, 2021

OVER TO YOU

I gave my heart over to you
when faced with supporting—
    and respecting—
        your decision to die.

That is how much I love you.
It is the greatest gift I could give you.

You deserved to have the kind of death you wanted.
I was determined to create that sacred space for you.

It was the most difficult thing
    I have ever done in my life.

It was the most beautiful thing
    I have ever witnessed.

The smile that crept onto your face,
    the gentle thunderstorm,
        followed by a rainbow

told me everything I needed to know
    about your death
    and restored my broken heart
        if only briefly.

March 20, 2021

NONETHELESS

The cold wind of death

blew upon me
one July day

though it did not
come for me

the result was the same
nonetheless

March 20, 2021

MOMENTS

It is in those

Silent
Still
Moments
that
Calm
Resides

and
Fragile
Fragments
of
Peace
Abide.

March 23, 2021

SHE STAYS WITH ME

Even in this darkness
    she stays with me
watches over me
    keeps me safe

Saying:
    I am here.
    I am with you.

Now, go on.

March 25, 2021

TENDER DAY

It is a tender day
to be out and about
in this post-Katy world.

April 3, 2021

WHAT I DON'T HAVE

I may have some days
that are better than others.

What I don't have
are any days that are as good
as the days I had
with you.

April 18, 2021

BARREN LAND

I stand exposed—
vulnerable
with no place to turn
for comfort
for love
for strength.

The life that she—
my beautiful
wonderous love—
shared with me
ended

the moment she died.

Since then,
I stand
on barren land.

June 13, 2021

LIFELINE

I wish I could call you, talk to you, check in with you—see what movies or TV shows you are watching or hear about what you are reading online or your current book. I wish I could call and hear your voice, hear you say you love me, how much you miss me—and we would reassure one another that it is only for the weekend, that is all, and we would not want to hang up because we missed each other so much, and I couldn't wait to get home to you. I was comforted knowing you were there when I was here. But now you are not there and I cannot call to hear your voice, hear you say you love me and miss me. I miss you so much, Katy. I do not want you to be gone. I want you here with me now, *please*.

June 18, 2021

JULY – DECEMBER

2021

YEAR ONE

Rattle around in a life without you
is all I seem to do.

One year. My sweetie. Good God.
How can you be gone?

July 3, 2021

LEFT UNDONE

Today, I discovered that the restaurant
where we had our first dinner date
    is no longer there.

I then realized we will never
go out for dinner together again.

We will never go
to *our* movie theater again.

We will never order in
our favorite foods again.

We will never travel
to new or familiar places again.

We will never sit
on our front porch together again.

There are so many things I miss doing
with you, and still so many things
    left undone.

July 6, 2021

OUR SIGNAL

I was lying in bed just now, listening
to the rain and dozing off here and there.
I was on my right side, so my back was to
Katy's side of the bed.

Simultaneously, I felt a light push
against my left shoulder just as a rumble
of thunder sounded.

I said, "Hi, sweetie. I love you. I miss you.
Thank you for letting me know you are here."
I smiled, eyes closed, still listening to the rain as
it started falling harder.

The gentle push on the shoulder is something
we used to do—usually in the morning—
when we wanted the other one to turn over
or come to the other side of the bed
so we could snuggle in together.

We also talked—before she died—
about her touching me gently like that
to let me know she is nearby.

What a wonderful feeling, that gentle push.

July 14, 2021

SMALL THINGS

I pull open the desk drawer,
    unsuspecting.

There sits her wallet,
    the wallet she will never hold again.

Pain and sadness consume me
when just moments ago
    all seemed calm.

Small things,
like seeing her wallet
or her favorite clothes she will never wear again
or the toothbrush she will never use again,

are hiding everywhere—
in closets, in drawers, or often
    in plain sight.

These small things cause big eruptions
for which I rarely seem prepared.

Yet somehow, I
reluctantly, surprisingly
    survive.

July 26, 2021

THAT IN-BETWEEN PLACE

Katy visited me overnight.

Not in a dream, but that in-between place,
where you are mostly asleep but kind of awake.
I saw her face. I notice when she comes to me
like that, I talk out loud. Although I am
mostly asleep, I hear myself talking.

"Hi, sweetie," I said.
        She didn't respond.
I asked her if she was okay.
        One of her eyes opened a little.
I asked her what was wrong.
        No response.
Then I asked her if she missed me.
        She scrunched up her face in a
        particularly endearing way and slightly nodded yes.

I said, "Oh, sweetie! It's okay. I'm right here."

I don't remember any more after that—
except for that sweet look on her face,
how tender she seemed, that I miss
seeing her face every day—and how happy
my heart was to see her again.

July 28, 2021

RESTING

Of all the things I could be doing,
    or should be doing,
I do none.

Instead, I crawl into bed and spend hours there,

letting my mind and body
    rest
under grief's weight.

And feeling guilty for doing so.

Society diminishes the need to rest
with demands to

keep
    doing
keep
    moving
keep
    going.

But sometimes
    resting
is the only thing
    grief allows me to do.

September 3, 2021

EACH DAY

Each day
each step
moves me further
into the Unknown.

The further away
time takes me from you
the more I want
time to Stop.

The Unknown
is not a place
I want to go
without you.

September 18, 2021

WITNESSING HER LAST BREATH

Her breathing had become ragged.
I was running around the room
opening windows,
as it had started raining.

She loved the rain.

Midway between windows—
one ear on her breathing,
the other on the rain—
she stopped.

I stopped.

I was at the end of the bed,
near her feet.
I looked at her, waiting.
She made no more sound.
Her chest was still.

I stood in shock—
dazed, bewildered

Suspended.

Holding my own breath,
until I was certain.

Witnessing her last breath
was the most powerful, beautiful, heartbreaking,
moving, devastating, wondrous experience
of my life.

October 21, 2021

EVERY TIME

I miss you

every time
I do something
we used to do.

That means

I miss you
always.

November 11, 2021

I KNOW HOW THIS SONG ENDS

I don't want to go through
another fall and winter
    without you.

It's all too empty, too painful,
too lonely, too dark
    outside and within.

I don't want to go through
a year of Seconds—

it only leads to a year of Thirds
    and Fourths
    and Fifths
        and on and on
like a broken record
for a broken soul.

I know how this song ends.
I don't need to hear it anymore.

November 12, 2021

UNMOORED

The fog of grief
is thick today.

Unmoored,
the wailing wall
remains unseen
until impact.

Although this fog
may lift

I never want you
to fade away.

November 18, 2021

HER VOICE

This morning, I was in a very deep sleep
when I clearly heard Katy say my name.

It was the tone she used when she was
trying to wake me up in the morning.

It took a couple of moments to register—
then I startled awake.

I looked around for her—like she
would be in bed right next to me.

She wasn't—but I heard her.
I knew she had been there.

I heard her beautiful voice
that I always loved.

In that moment
it was all that mattered.

November 23, 2021

LAST AND FIRST

Every Last
is as momentous as
Every First.

Every First
is a reminder of the
Original Last.

December 4, 2021

WHEN YOU WERE REAL

When you were real
and here with me

and I could touch
the softness of your skin
and I could feel
the warmth of your embrace
and I could hear
the sweetness of your laugh
and I could rest my head on your shoulder
and feel safe in your arms
and know that with you
my life has found meaning
and we could turn to one another
in times of challenge and heartache

when you were real
and here with me

I knew I was home.

December 5, 2021

DOING THINGS ALONE

It is hard to do some things alone,
impossible to do most others.

Where there were two, now there is one—
a gaping lack of presence is of no help.

                                        December 15, 2021

LOVED

I will
I will carry
I will carry you always in my heart

I will
I will carry you
I will
I will keep
I will keep you always in my heart

I will
I will keep you
I will carry
I will keep
I will
I will hold
I will hold you always in my heart

I will
I will hold you
I will carry
I will keep
I will hold
I will

In my heart
I will cherish
I will honor
I will remember
In my heart, you will always be

Carried
Kept
Held
Cherished
Honored
Remembered

Loved.

December 20, 2021

EVEN AFTER

In the end
it is always only love
that matters most,
that binds our hearts—
    to carry one another
    to give shelter in the storm
    to comfort in the tender moments

even after death parts us.

Perhaps
especially then.

December 27, 2021

JANUARY – JUNE

2022

A FOUND LIST POEM

write/email accountant
call irs
email update to attorney
call hh
scream

                                             January 5, 2022

GRIEF

has many faces

it holds you prisoner

it settles in your bones
becoming all that holds you together

it is a curiously deceptive creature

you go on your way as best you can
then you step in a hole of sorrow

it might swallow you whole
or you might just stumble
      barely missing a beat

but it is still there
silently undermining
any hope of lasting stability

it is relentless
ruthless
and arbitrary

in the ways it brings you to your knees
begging for relief
from the many faces of
Grief.

January 6, 2022

THANKS FOR ASKING

Angry
Tired
Depressed
Heartbroken
Frustrated
Irritable
Restless
Lost
Foggy
Scattered
Protective
Judged
Private
Abandoned
Pressured
Broken

is how I feel.

Thanks for asking.

January 14, 2022

NO FAIR

I watched you go
when I wanted you to stay.

Death does not
play fair.

January 26, 2022

TIME ZONES

One year and seven months ago today,
Katy died.

She has been gone that long.
Yet for me, it just happened.

Grief creates a whole new time zone—
one you share with the rest of the world
and one that is made just for you—
the moment your loved one dies.

I, as the griever,
can still enter the Rest-of-the-World Time Zone,
though it can be a challenging undertaking.

But the Rest-of-the-World Time Zone
denies the existence of the Grief Time Zone.

The Rest-of-the-World Time Zone goes on—
with only a short-term ripple effect

from the devastation that established
the Grief Time Zone—

where Time is frozen and slow to thaw.

February 3, 2022

HOW I KNOW

On the hardest of days,
    when sorrows, worries, and struggles
        come the strongest,
I think of Katy—
    eyes closed, no longer
    consciously communicating
    with anyone in this world,

her head turned up slightly—
    her face bright and attentive,
        nodding *yes* to someone or something
            only she could see—

That is how I know she is okay
    and I can rest.

                                            February 8, 2022

A PLACE TO LAND

Sliding
down
the rope that
hangs me

Dangling
between
a rock and
a dark place

Scraping raw
the wounds
of your death

In life,
you raised me up

With your love,
I became more

Now,
I am left

sliding
dangling
scraping—

Looking
for a sliver
of your light
on which
to land.

February 17, 2022

COME HOME

Lately, out of the blue,
I expect you to walk
through the back door—
like this was all a mistake.

My heart fills up
with so much joy at
the thought of seeing you
one more time.

Please, come home.

February 19, 2022

SURPRISE PASSENGER

On my way down to see family last Sunday
I suddenly felt Katy's hand
resting on my leg—
something we used to do when
traveling in the car together.

It was so nice to have her with me.

March 16, 2022

FOUR WORDS

I realized, after checking
the "Widow" box
for the first time, that

I am a widow.

Four words I never
thought I would say.

Four words that
shattered my world.

Four words that
make it too damn
official.

March 31, 2022

WHEN GRIEF INDUCES SILENCE

The space
between
the silence

Is fertile soil
in which to
spin tales
and non-truths.

Use the silence
that grief induces
to reflect

not project.

June 5, 2022

THE FAILURE OF LANGUAGE

Language fails us
when it comes to grief.

It hinders and impedes
our words
from finding meaning—

from fully expressing
the experience we need
so desperately to voice.

Instead,
we remain silent
noncommittal
or compliant
with other people's discomfort.

The failure of language
keeps us needlessly bound
to our grief.

June 9, 2022

WHY I STOPPED

She asked me once,
    a long time ago,
why I stopped
    writing poetry.

I didn't know how to answer her then.

Reflecting on it now,
if I could answer
that question today,
    I would say

Because I was happy.

June 16, 2022

BLAZING TRUTH

This is a brand-new car.
One you have never been in.
Yet when I moved my hand
to rest it where your thigh would be,
I felt you there with such intensity—
like a jolt of current
straight to the core of me—
blazing into me the understanding:
    you *are* always with me.

June 17, 2022

MOMENTARY REPRIEVE

But when my eyes land
    on a picture of you

my face cannot help but light up
my heart cannot help but feel full
my soul cannot help but come alive

Until

my tears fall freely again,
remembering you are no longer here with me.

June 20, 2022

JULY – DECEMBER

2022

EVERYTHING'S CHANGED

That was my first thought
as I got out of bed this morning.

Like the reality of—
the implications of—
Katy's death
were just hitting me
two years later.

Maybe it's just on a deeper level.

Grief seems to burrow down
to depths I never knew
existed.

July 8, 2022

LAKE HARRIET

This is my spiritual home.

Although we did not meet here,
we may as well have.

We both walked this lake
with others—before
we found one another.

But once we did, it became our lake.

We spent a lot of time here.

We first lived together
right up the street—
one long block from the water's edge.

It will always remind me
of you, of us—and our life together.

I come here to remember.
I come here to feel close to you.
I come here to write, to cry, or just be.

I know you come here too.
I see and feel you everywhere.

July 20, 2022

THE CONSTANT QUESTIONS

What if
If only
Would have
Could have
Should have

would not
have changed
a thing.

Spare yourself
the agony
these questions bring.

The outcome
would be the same
no matter how much
you try to change
the narrative.

July 21, 2022

SINCE YOU'VE GONE

The four phrases
I say a lot:

I love you.

I miss you.

I'm sorry.

Please, come back.

July 26, 2022

I FEEL

I feel lost.

Stripped down
to my
absolute
barest,

I feel alone.

Standing in this world
on
my
own,

I feel the

complete
total
loss

of you.

August 1, 2022

THE COMFORT OF YOU

I have photos
that show me
>   your sparkling eyes
>   your beautiful face
>   your inviting smile

And I cannot help but smile back at you.

But I do not ever
want to forget your body—
>   the softness of your skin
>   the gentleness of your touch
>   the warmth of your embrace.

Photos do not fully capture

>   the comfort of you.

August 29, 2022

UNWILLING TO LAND

I continue to live a life

untethered
disconnected
unwilling

to land
in a world
without
you.

September 22, 2022

GRIEF EVENT

I had a very intense grief event—
like I haven't had in a while.

Wishing I was gone,
wishing Katy would come back,
    wailing
    sobbing
    pleading,

I finally forced myself
to get under the weighted blanket.

It helped comfort me.

I ended up having a dream
with Katy in it—
so real I thought for sure
I would see her next to me
when I woke during the night.

She wasn't, but at least
she visited me in the dream.

It was enough to settle me.

                                       September 23, 2022

LIVING AND DYING

It is true
that dying
is a part of
living.

It is equally true
that living
is a part of
dying.

Neither happens
in a vacuum.

October 2, 2022

NEXT TIME

We will meet each other
    sooner

We will love each other
    longer

And we will live to old age
    together

October 5, 2022

EMPTY MESS

This uncharacteristic mess
around me
tries to fill
the emptiness
of a house
without
you.

                                        October 7, 2022

THEN, NOW, ALWAYS

You are
the sweetheart
of my soul.

You are
the magic
of my life.

You are
the rainbow
of my days.

You are
the love of my life
and the life of my love.

Then,
Now,
Always.

October 17, 2022

LIVING GRIEF

The first year,
I felt my grief.

Since then,
I have been living it.

I have learned that
grief is not something
you get over or move on from.

Grief simply becomes
a part of your life,
but not all of who you are.

It walks with you, always.
It is not a one-and-done.
Nor is grief an enemy to be conquered.

Grief embraces you—
whether or not you
      embrace it in return—

And it stays with you
like a necessary guest
you need to accommodate.

October 18, 2022

WHAT IF IT IS

Can I be happy
with the memory of you?

Can the time we had together
be enough?

Can your memory sustain me
in a world without you?

Can it be enough to settle my soul
and calm my heart?

Can I trust the memory of you won't die
like you did?

But you are always in my heart
and I am always in yours.

We made certain we each knew that before you left.

Can I be happy with you in my heart
and me in yours?

Can that knowledge be enough
to keep me from breaking?

To bring me back
from the loss that is you?

And most terrifying of all:
what if it is.

October 23, 2022

SENSE AND SENSELESS

You opened me up
to a sense of self
I never knew.

Your death
has left me
senseless.

October 28, 2022

YOUR PHONE

When I hold your phone
I see you

holding it
walking with it
using it
playing with it
    texting
    calling
    reading
    surfing

When I hold your phone
I see you

no longer a phone
    call away.

October 28, 2022

ALL THE WAYS

Your death
took away
my breath

and showed me
all the ways
we break.

                                                  November 4, 2022

WHAT IT HAS ALWAYS BEEN

Do not tamp down
your tears.
Do not stifle
your sobs.
Give yourself
completely
over to your
Grief.
Do not push it
away
or allow others
to push you into
doing the same.
They have no
authority
over you,
nor have they
understanding
of your
Grief.
The only way
is through
and even then
it is not done,
it simply becomes
what it has
always been—
the love you feel
for the one
who died.

November 4, 2022

GRIEF DOES NOT EXPIRE

Contrary
to popular belief
grief
does not have
an expiration date.

Each day
each season
each year
only brings
different ways
for grief
to show
itself.

Grief does not expire.
It merely ages
alongside us.

November 22, 2022

SHE SAID

"I need you to be stronger than you have ever been in your life."

She knew her dying was going to break my heart.
But she did not want it to break me.

So, I used her words to guide me:

When I was on my knees wailing.
When I screamed and sobbed into my pillow.
When I wanted to join her.
When it hurt to breathe.
When I missed her with every ounce of my being.
When I did not know how I could or why I should go on without her.
When the emptiness of life without her engulfed me.
When there was no place to go with my grief.
When I had to do something without her for the first, fifth, or fiftieth time.
When I reached for her in the middle of the night and she was not there.
When I could not deal with one. more. thing.
When regrets, questions, and wonderings caused unnecessary suffering.
When I needed so badly for her to walk in the back door after work so we could greet each other with a hello, a hug, a kiss.

When I look around and only find her in my memory—
                and the words she said.

December 3, 2022

THROUGH THE FOG

My heart aches
and then it breaks

Even the air
touching my skin
hurts too much

Looking through
the fog of grief

I see you everywhere.

December 17, 2022

JANUARY – JULY

2023

LIFE

Life
is getting
in the way
of my grief.

Does it
not understand
the toll of
Grief's demands?

January 7, 2023

BECAUSE

I wish I never had to say goodbye to you.
I wish I had gone with you.

It's so hard and lonely here without you.
It's no fun here without you.

I just want us to be together again.
I just want to be with you because

I love you

and

we still had a lot of living to do.

January 27, 2023

SOME DAYS

Some days
I can only do
one
small
thing.

One step
one task
one
small
breath.

Some days
that
one
small
thing

allows me
to do the
next
small
thing.

Some days
that
one
small
breath

is all
I can
manage.

February 4, 2023

NEGOTIATING NEW SPACES

It felt like Katy was asleep
right next to me this morning.

She was to my left.
I was sleeping on her side
of the bed, on my back.

I remember thinking
it was nice, comforting
to feel her there.

She usually only comes
when I sleep on my side of the bed.

Maybe we are learning
to negotiate these new spaces
together.

February 10, 2023

NO OTHER WORD

Fuck
Fuck
Fuck
Fuck
Fuck

Because sometimes
no other word
will do.

February 23, 2023

RETREAT

Being here, on the North Shore,
has opened up a place in my heart
where words dwell.

It has brought me back
to the place where I am firmly anchored
in creation.

Be it the waves
chasing one another
to shore,

Or my pen meeting paper,
words flowing as freely
as the water.

At times, the lake is calm,
like a soul in silent reflection.

At times, the lake is rough,
like a restless spirit in turmoil.

Today, the lake is like my grief in full rampage—
my battered heart pounding against the shore
that once was our life together.

March 16, 2023

ONLY ME

I sit
where you used to sit

I sleep
where you used to sleep

I go
to places we used to go

I do
the things we planned to do

I cook
what we used to eat

I wear
the clothes we always shared

I listen
to the music we both enjoyed

I watch
the shows we used to watch

I read
in bed like we always did

I do all these things
because

I want
to be us

But I am
only me.

March 20, 2023

SELFISH QUESTIONS

Do you miss me?

I know you weren't afraid to die
but do you wish you hadn't?

Do you wish you had more time?
Assuming the strokes had not happened.
I wish they hadn't.

I wish you weren't taken
from the me-of-we so soon.
Do you regret leaving me?
Do you wish you could come back?

Selfish questions, I know.

Now that I put those words to paper,
I hope you don't have regrets.

Then again, I believe you are in a place of
infinite knowledge and understanding.
Regrets fall into place when everything is
taken into consideration.

Still,
do you miss me?

April 29, 2023

MANY MORE

Our wedding anniversary is today

Nine years legal—
six when you died

I still do not know
how that part is real

I only know
I want many more
lifetimes
with you

May 2, 2023

THE PROJECTOR OF GRIEF

is on constant replay
    with a piercing zoom lens
    that misses nothing

events, conversations,
passing comments—

many of which were insignificant in the moment
    or resolved at the time—

explode to the surface

along with those things you meant to
get back to or talk about later

but time ran out

and that projector
    with its piercing zoom lens
    and constant replay

seems to focus on things
    that break our hearts even more
or cause doubt
    where none existed before
or make us question
    what we have always known to be true

all without valid reason
all because grief messes with
reality by playing with our minds

the projector of grief
    is a decoy

it distracts us from feeling our true loss:
    the death of our loved one

and from realizing the true source of our guilt:
    being the one who lived

one of the hardest—
    yet most freeing and loving—
tasks of grief

is learning to turn that projector off.

June 20, 2023

GRATITUDE

Thank you for visiting me in my sleep last night, Katy.

It was very comforting that you came to me
        at this time of change.

I loved getting to spend
        a little more time in this house
            with you.

June 24, 2023

THE NATURE OF LOSS

Today I saw an SUV that reminded me of one you had many years ago. It made me smile. Later, when I was walking to my car after leaving a store, I saw a woman who looked like you—so much so that it stopped me in my tracks. I was stunned. For several moments, I felt joy in my heart at the thought that you were still here, alive!

Then reality settled back in.

It had been a while since I last experienced anything like that. At some point, without my knowledge, I got used to walking around in the muted state of grief—rotely going through life—until something like this comes along and jolts me into remembering just how happy I would be if you were here.

But reality always settles back in.

That is the nature of loss.

June 27, 2023

MOVING

I just realized when I go up north this time,
I won't be coming back here to our home.

Our home here will be gone.

The last place we both lived.

The place that holds twelve years of memories—
    our grandkids
    our families
    our friends
    our neighbors

The place where your life ended.

I know our home will still be intact,
just located in a different place.

Although it may have one less occupant,
it will always be filled with you and me.

Thank you for leading me to it.

July 2, 2023

LOSING KATY

The journey to your death began three years ago, in early June.

Overnight, you almost fully recovered from the first stroke. It might have been a mini stroke. But it still took its toll, leaving you exhausted throughout each day.

After that first stroke, we had many deep conversations, rereading health documents and confirming what we do and do not want in the event of medical emergencies. We reviewed our end-of-life wishes.

We cried and held each other close at night.

COVID still had many things locked down, especially in medical settings. I had to wait in the car while you went in, alone, to have an MRI. It was agony not being able to go in with you. I watched helplessly as you disappeared from my sight.

What was I going to do if I lost you completely?

When you came out, you described how abandoned the hospital felt. Large areas were partitioned off. You said you had to be escorted to and from the MRI department due to the maze created by the closures of hallways and spaces. You said no one else was around.

You found it profoundly disturbing.

Ten days after the first stroke, you had the second one. This one struck at the core of you. It affected your ability to communicate, to speak, which was an essential component of *you*. It was not only how you connected to others, but to life itself.

COVID limited your options, but I suspect you would have made the same decisions regardless. Being able to interact fully was a significant necessity to your quality of life. I knew that. We had talked about it several times over the years. Jarring as it was, I knew what your decision would be.

No treatment.

Hospice was brought in for the last two and a half weeks of your life. We were both relieved when they came. No more needless suffering and worrying for you. Still, it was by no means smooth sailing. Dying is a labor similar to giving birth.

I think, as you lay unconscious, you were setting everything right in your life, in a way that did not or could not happen while alive—paving the way for a smooth transition to your next destination and arriving with a clarity of Presence.

That is my belief, anyway.

The journey to your death ended three years ago this evening.

One month to the day from your first stroke.

You were at home the whole time. We were together the whole time. If I had to lose you, how could it possibly be any other way? We were, after all, always at our best—together.

July 3, 2023

Katy Heffelfinger and Jackie Disch on what would be their last vacation. North Shore of Lake Superior, February, 2020. This selfie is the last photo of them together.

NOTES AND ACKNOWLEDGMENTS

I am not the only person in Katy's life to face a loss when she died. Katy was a mother, a grandmother, and a sister; an aunt, a cousin, and an in-law; a friend, a colleague, and a mentor. All of these relations have suffered the loss of her loving, gentle, funny, compassionate Being. I can only write about my own grief, but I want to acknowledge theirs. Katy loved and was loved by many.

A special thank-you to Donna Biedron, Lyndall Johnson, Susan Gamble, and Kristen Johnson, who agreed to be beta readers for *Losing Katy*. Your love, support, and understanding came through in the beautiful, insightful feedback each of you provided. I am grateful for your friendships. Katy would be so proud and happy that you all helped make this book a reality. An additional thank you to Lyndall for inspiring the back cover description of *Losing Katy*.

To the person who wished to remain anonymous: You have meant a great deal to both Katy and me. Much love and gratitude to you.

Thank you to the team at BookLogix for helping with the heavy lifting that bringing a book to life requires.

And to you—the reader. Thank you for choosing this book out of all the possible books available today. I truly hope you found something in this story that you can relate to, that is helpful to you, or perhaps provides some comfort to you. We each experience grief in our own way, but grief itself is universal.

None of us are alone.

Other Books by
JACKIE L. DISCH

Hitting Bone

Life Forces a Journey

www.ingramcontent.com/pod-product-compliance
Lightning Source LLC
Chambersburg PA
CBHW060612080526
44585CB00013B/798